Japanes Cookbook

MW01289481

Favorite Japanese Takeout
Recipes to Make at Home

Lina Chang

Copyrights

Disclaimer and Terms of Use

Effort has been made to ensure that the information in this book is accurate and complete. However, the author and the publisher do not warrant the accuracy of the information, text, and graphics contained within the book due to the rapidly changing nature of science, research, known and unknown facts, and internet. The author and the publisher do not hold any responsibility for errors, omissions, or contrary interpretation of the subject matter herein. This book is presented solely for motivational and informational purposes only.

The recipes provided in this book are for informational purposes only and are not intended to provide dietary advice. A medical practitioner should be consulted before making any changes in diet. Additionally, recipe cooking times may require adjustment depending on age and quality of appliances. Readers are strongly urged to take all precautions to ensure ingredients are fully cooked in order to avoid the dangers of foodborne illnesses. The recipes and suggestions provided in this book are solely the opinion of the author. The author and publisher do not take any responsibility for any consequences that may result due to following the instructions provided in this book.

ISBN: 978-1537674506

Printed in the United States

Contents

Introduction

Japanese food has lured Americans away from the usual meat and potato meals and French-style creamy dishes of the past, and its easy availability through takeout has brought this exotic cuisine closer to the everyday Joe, further enriching the multicultural American palate. Japanese food is rich in culture, being recognized by the UN for it cultural significance. It has introduced the concept of *umami* to the Western world. Umami may be translated as "rich, savory taste" that the Japanese consider as the fifth basic taste along with bitter, sweet, salty, and sour. Like other takeout dishes in America, original traditions and flavors have given way to alterations in order to cater to American taste buds. Some feel that *Washoku*, or the purest and most traditional Japanese cuisine, has been lost in Japanese takeout in America. The emphasis on simplicity and respect for the five basic flavors has been replaced by vibrant and what others might consider flamboyant flavors of Japanese-American takeout. But this blending perhaps reflects the dynamic traits of American culture such as diversity and adaptability.

Japanese cooking is recognized for its healthfulness because it is rich in plant-based ingredients and is sparing in the use of oil. However, due to time constraints and economic reasons, fresh ingredients are now being replaced with canned and processed substitutes.

Fish and vegetables have always formed the greater part of Japanese cuisine. Only around the 19th century did the Japanese begin to use large cuts of meat in their dishes, resulting in tasty recipes such as *Katsudon* (fried breaded pork cutlet). Being masters of innovation, the Japanese are known to take the best from other cultures and incorporate them in their own. Their dishes are also marked by influences from China in their dumpling and noodle dishes, and from other cultures in dishes such as curries, burgers, and steaks.

It is not exactly known when Japanese restaurants were first established in the US. It is likely that visiting Japanese businessmen knew where to find familiar fare as early as the 1950s, but Japanese food only began to be recognized around the 1960s. Sushi restaurants in Little Tokyo, Los Angeles, began to gain popularity especially among the Hollywood crowd. Other restaurants were soon also put up in cities like New York and Chicago, until sushi became the rage by the 1980s.

Sushi refers to the vinegared, seasoned rice on which raw fish is placed. As raw fish was still not well-received at first, resourceful chefs thought of using local produce that would be more acceptable to the American palate. The California Maki was thus invented. This invention is credited to a Canadian chef named Hidekazu Tojo, who thought of substituting fatty fish with avocado during the 1970s. Today, more and more creations have emerged, putting Western ingredients in an originally Eastern dish, resulting in a fascinating fusion of flavors.

Ingredients in Japanese Cuisine

Japanese ingredients were originally seasonal – for freshness and to welcome the coming of each new season. Although a wide variety of ingredients are used, below are the ones you are sure to find in Japanese cooking.

Noodles

Here some commonly used noodles in Japanese cooking.
1. Ramen – Noodles of Chinese origin, made from wheat and kansui, a natural and nutritious salt that lends the yellowish color to the noodles. These may be thin or curly and thick.
2. Soba – Healthy, often gluten-free buckwheat noodles. Some may contain small amounts of wheat.
3. Somen – Extremely thin wheat noodles popularly eaten cold in hot weather. It is also eaten in hot broth as nyumen.
4. Yaki Udon – Thin, curly wheat noodles that are stir-fried rather than cooked in broth.
5. Udon – Thick, versatile wheat noodles that absorb flavors well. Can be eaten hot or cold, dry (stir-fried) or in broth.
6. Shirataki – Gelatinous noodles made from konjac yam. Popularly used for sukiyaki.

Rice

Japanese rice is the staple and is present in every meal. Other rice varieties may not be suitable for Japanese cooking. Japanese rice is best for sushi because of its stickiness and ability to absorb moisture.

Rice Wine

Rice wines like *sake* and *mirin* are used to add flavor. Rice cooked with rice wine becomes more flavorful and shiny in appearance. Although both are rice wines, *mirin* is sweeter and contains less alcohol. To substitute sake for *mirin*, a little sugar must be added.

Seafood

Fish and other seafood are highly prized by the Japanese and freshness is a must. Japanese chefs are trained to choose the best and freshest fish. The Japanese eat a variety of produce from the sea. Tuna, salmon, mackerel, sardines, and herring are just some fish ingredients that are used. Bonito flakes or *katsuobushi* are dried tuna chips used as flavoring or garnish to give *umami* (a pleasant savory sensation considered as the "fifth taste") to dishes.

Soy Sauce

To come up with the right flavor in a Japanese dish, one needs to master the use of authentic Japanese soy sauce in combination with other ingredients. There are two types – *koikuchi* and *usukuchi*. Koikuchi is dark in color while usukuchi is light in color but saltier.

Vegetables

Vegetables and herbs in season are widely used in Japanese dishes. Some popular ingredients are *daikon*, cucumber, carrots, onions, and green leafy vegetables. Beans, nuts, seeds, and mushrooms are also used. Again, freshness is the most important consideration. Seaweed, though taken from the sea, is classified as a vegetable and is used to flavor soup stocks, as toppings, and as an ingredient for salads. Edible seaweed like *wakame, nori* (laver or seaweed "paper") and *kombu* (kelp) are some commonly used ingredients.

Common Tools and Equipment

The basic tools and equipment found in any Western kitchen are adequate for Japanese cooking. Here are some other tools worth considering to save time and to make food preparation easier.

Rice cooker
Since rice is the staple Japanese food, this can be very helpful. There are several models with different functions but the most basic will do.

Hangiri
A wooden container for storing rice. This is needed by those who intend to make sushi frequently. The wood allows the rice to sweat, so it doesn't spoil as easily as it would in a metal or glass container.

Wok
The Japanese also use the wok for deep-frying and stir-frying. A flat bottomed one may be more stable and efficient. A heavy frying pan will also do.

Sushi rolling mat (Makisu)
A must for rolling your sushi. These are made of bamboo tied with cotton string.

Stove-top grill
This will make grilling more convenient. A heavy cast iron stove-top grill is good for cooking over a gas flame. This is a good replacement for the Japanese indoor grill called the *yakiami*.

Cooking chopsticks (Saibashi)

These are long, unlacquered, and tied with a string at the ends. Good for fishing out pieces of food when frying, turning, stirring, or arranging food for serving.

Drop-lid (Otoshibuta)

A wooden lid used when simmering to keep liquid in and prevent large bubbles from forming. It allows steam to escape around its side as it is not a tight-fitting type of lid and simply "floats" over the simmering contents of the pot. It helps food to develop flavor while cooking and also helps delicate ingredients to retain their shape.

Cooking Methods

The Japanese want to keep their cooking as simple as possible to best preserve the freshness of the ingredients. They make use of four basic cooking methods:

Frying (Agemono)

This involves deep-frying in cooking oil and is the method used to make dishes like *tempura* and *tonkatsu*. This method is said to have been introduced by the Chinese and the Portuguese.

Steaming (Mushimono)

Traditional Japanese cooking is sparing in the use of oil, so many foods are cooked in a bamboo basket over simmering water. One popular steamed dish is *chawan mushi*, a custard with vegetables and chicken. In this case, the cups holding the custard are placed in a layer of water inside a covered pan to cook.

Boiling (Nimono)

Many dishes are boiled or simmered, sometimes all in one pot. Popular boiled or simmered dishes are *sukiyaki* (beef with vegetables), *yoseNabe* (seafood and vegetables) and *yudofo* (bean curd).

Broiling (Yakimono)

Many meats and seafood are broiled, such as *shioyaki* (skewered salted fish) and *teriyaki* (broiled meat in a sweetened sauce).

Though some recipes in this cookbook try to retain as much authenticity as possible, the needs and preferences of the modern American cook are also taken into consideration. This compilation of popular Japanese-American takeout dishes contains recipes that have been simplified as much as possible and modified so that the ordinary home cook can easily find the ingredients and prepare them using basic kitchen equipment; with the assurance of impressive results.

Bento Boxes

Bento refers to home-packed meals placed in lunch boxes in Japan. Traditionally, a bento box would contain rice, fish or meat, and vegetables or pickles. The contents of the box are meant not only to be tasty and nutritious, but appealing to the eye as well.

Nowadays, Japanese restaurants offer bento boxes, offering complete meals in a box. Each partition is filled with a different kind of dish. The bento box eases the difficulty in choosing food combinations to order and can be taken home to enjoy a restaurant meal there, or taken to the office or school for lunch or dinner.

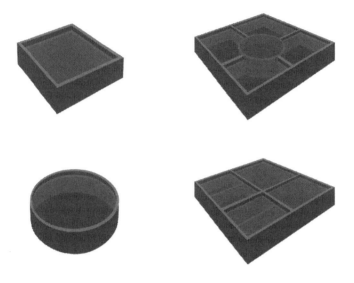

To make your own bento box, here are some considerations:

- Choose a box appropriate for your needs. A large box would not be suitable for a person who eats like a bird. Determine the amount of food to be eaten. Dieters can use this to their advantage for controlling portion size. The traditional boxes may hold portions that may be too little or too much for you. Look around for other containers that are suitable.

- Play with colors, textures, shapes, and flavors. It can be a fun way to mix and match foods to come up with an edible work of art. Sushi is particularly appealing to the eye and you can put a variety of flavors in a box. You can use cookie cutters to make heart- or star-shaped *nigiri* or sushi.

- Pack the food tightly, especially when using a box without partitions, to prevent shifting or spillage. Food like lettuce, celery, or carrots can also be used to separate the food. Start with solid, bulky items first, then insert flexible items into the spaces left. Brightly colored items inserted in spaces can serve as accents and give a more attractive overall appearance. Small containers can also be used to hold some items; those with lids can be used for sauces, dips, and soup.

- Determine the proportion of each type of food you intend to pack. There are traditional proportions followed (such as 4:3:2:1 for rice: side dish: vegetables: pickles or dessert) but you can set your own proportions based on your own requirements. This could be a good way to proportion one's intake of carbs, protein and fiber, for instance. Using the recipes in this book, you can come up with different combinations. Here are just a few suggestions:

  - An all-sushi bento with a seafood roll, a vegetable roll and a meat roll.
  - A meal combination containing an appetizer, soup, a salad, a main dish and dessert.
  - A combination of tempura, sushi, soup, and a salad or pickles (if there'sspace, you can add a small dessert).
  - An all-seafood bento.
  - An all-vegetable bento.

The possibilities are endless!

Let's now fill up these bento boxes with delicious food. Let's get cooking!

Appetizers

Steamed Green Soybean (Edamame)

Serves: 3-4
Preparation Time: 5 minutes
Cooking Time: 3-5 minutes

Ingredients
1 ½-2 cups edamame in the pod, topped and tailed,
fresh or frozen
2 ½ tablespoons sea salt, divided
Water, for boiling

Directions

1. Soak the edamame in hot water for about 5 minutes. Drain and rinse.
2. Rub the pods with about 1 tablespoon of salt.
3. In a medium saucepan, boil enough water to cover edamame. Stir in the remaining salt.
4. Boil the edamame for 3-5 minutes, or until it floats to the surface. Remove the pot from the heat and drain out the water.
5. Spread the edamame on a tray in one layer to cool. You may use a fan for faster cooling.
6. Squeeze the pods with a thumb and forefinger to pop the beans out of the pod.
7. Serve. (Do not eat the pod.)

Dumplings (Gyoza)

Serves: 10
Preparation Time: 30 minutes
Cooking Time: 15 minutes

Ingredients
1 (10 ounce) package wonton wrappers
1 tablespoon vegetable oil
¼ cup water

For filling
1 tablespoon sesame oil
2 cups cabbage, chopped
½ small onion, chopped
1 clove garlic, chopped
¼ cup carrot, chopped
1 cup minced pork (minced chicken, beef, or seafood may also be used)
1 egg, beaten

Directions

1. In a large skillet, heat the sesame oil over medium-high heat.
2. In the sesame oil, sauté the cabbage, onion, garlic, and carrot until the cabbage is tender and translucent.
3. Add the pork and egg, stirring constantly. Cook until the pork is browned. Remove from the heat and let it cool slightly.
4. To make the dumplings, place about a tablespoon of filling on the center of each wrapper and fold it in half to enclose the filling. Moisten the inner edges and pinch to seal.
5. In a large skillet, preheat the vegetable oil over medium-high heat.
6. Fry the *gyoza* until lightly browned (about 1 minute per side).
7. Add the water and cover the skillet. Let the dumplings steam until almost all the liquid has evaporated.
8. Serve with soy dipping sauce or spicy soy dipping sauce.

Vegetarian Gyoza

Serves: 12
Preparation Time: 30 minutes
Cooking Time: 15 minutes

Ingredients
1 (10 ounce) package wonton wrappers
24 lettuce leaves
2 tablespoons peanut oil, divided

For filling
Cooking spray
4 cups shiitake mushrooms, diced
4 cups cabbage, grated or finely chopped
2 tablespoons green onions, chopped
2 tablespoons *mirin*
2 tablespoons soy sauce
2 teaspoons fresh ginger, peeled and grated
½ teaspoon salt
¼ teaspoon dark sesame oil

3 cloves garlic, minced

Directions
1. Coat a large skillet with cooking spray and heat it over medium heat.
2. First, cook the mushrooms, stirring constantly, until the moisture evaporates.
3. Add the cabbage and cook until softened (about 3 minutes).
4. Stir in the rest of the ingredients for the filling and simmer for 2 minutes.
5. Remove from the heat and let it cool.
6. To make the dumplings, place about 2 teaspoons to a tablespoon of the filling on the center of each wrapper and fold it in half to enclose the filling. Moisten the inner edges, and pinch to seal.
7. In a large skillet, preheat the vegetable oil over medium-high heat.
8. Fry the *gyoza* until lightly browned (about 1 minute per side).
9. Add the water and cover the skillet. Let it steam until almost all the liquid has evaporated.
10. Serve with spicy dipping sauce or soy dipping sauce.

Fried Eggplant in Tempura Sauce (Agedashi Nasu)

Serves: 2
Preparation Time: 5-7 minutes
Cooking Time: 2-5 minutes

Ingredients
⅓ cup plus 1 tablespoon *dashi* stock or broth
1 ½ tablespoons soy sauce
1 tablespoon *mirin*
1 teaspoon sugar
Vegetable oil, for frying
2 medium-sized eggplants, destemmed, cut lengthwise and then crosswise
¾ cup hot water

1 tablespoon ginger, grated, for garnish
Chopped green onion and bonito flakes, for garnish (optional)

Directions
1. In a medium serving bowl, combine the stock or broth, soy sauce, *mirin*, and sugar. Set aside.
2. Make diagonal slits on the eggplant skins, about ⅛ inch apart and halfway into the eggplant. Pat the eggplants dry with paper towels.
3. Heat oil in a frying pan over medium heat, about 1-2 inches deep, to 350°F.
4. Deep fry the eggplant for 1 minute on each side, then remove it from the heat and place it in a metal rack or colander.
5. Pour the hot water over the eggplant to remove any excess oil.
6. Place the still-warm slices of eggplant in the *Dashi*-based stock.
7. Garnish with the grated ginger or green onion and bonito flakes (optional) and serve.

Japanese-Style Chicken Wings (Tebasaki)

Serves: 6
Preparation Time: 10 minutes
Cooking Time: 30 minutes

Ingredients:

1 cup flour

½ teaspoon white pepper powder

½ teaspoon garlic powder (optional)

½ teaspoon cayenne pepper, or to taste
2 eggs, beaten
3 pounds chicken wings, patted dry with paper towels
1 cup butter plus 2 tablespoons vegetable oil
Green onion, chopped, for garnish (optional)

For basting sauce
3 tablespoons soy sauce
3 tablespoons water
1 cup sugar (or ½ cup sugar plus honey, to taste)
½ cup white vinegar
½ teaspoon MSG (optional)
¼ teaspoon Chinese 5-spice powder (optional)
½ teaspoon salt

Directions

1. Combine the basting sauce ingredients in a bowl and set them aside.
2. Mix the flour and other dry ingredients together.
3. Dip the wings into the beaten eggs and then into the flour mixture.
4. Preheat the oven to 350°F.
5. Preheat butter and/or oil for frying in a heavy skillet over medium heat.
6. When butter/oil is hot, fry the wings until they are deep brown and crisp, then transfer them into a shallow roasting pan. Arrange them in a single layer.
7. Bake the wings for about 30 minutes, basting with the sauce and turning them over from time to time.
8. Serve garnished with chopped green onions (optional).

Marinated Runny Yolk Boiled Egg

Serves: 4
Preparation Time15 minutes plus 2 hours marinating time
Cooking Time: 7-7 ½ minutes

Ingredients
2 large eggs
Water for boiling
2 tablespoons vinegar
Ice water

For marinade
6 tablespoons dark soy sauce
1 teaspoon sugar
2 tablespoons Chinese cooking wine

Directions

1. Place the eggs in a bowl of warm water to avoid cracking due to the sudden temperature change when they are placed in boiling water.
2. Boil enough water in a small pot or saucepan to cover the eggs.
3. Add the vinegar to the boiling water.
4. Using a pin, puncture the base (the wider end) of the egg to further prevent cracking due to pressure while boiling.
5. Use a large spoon to gently place the eggs in the boiling water.
6. Simmer for 7 ½ minutes, or just 7 minutes for medium-sized eggs. The timing is crucial for getting the right texture of whites and yolks.
7. Immediately transfer the cooked eggs to the ice water. The eggs should cool down so the contents will separate from the shell and stay intact when shelled.
8. When the eggs have cooled, tap them all over to break the shell (do not peel them yet).
9. Combine the marinade ingredients and pour them in a container just the right size to keep the eggs in a single layer, while submerged as much as possible. Top up with water to submerge fully.
10. Cover with plastic wrap and marinate, refrigerated, for 2 hours to overnight.
11. Slice each egg in half and carefully remove it from the shell.
12. Sprinkle the yolks with a little bit of the marinade mixture, and serve.

Stewed Pork Appetizer (Chasu)

Serves: 3-4
Preparation Time: 5 minutes
Cooking Time: 1 hour 25 minutes

Ingredients
¾-1 pound pork belly block, skin or rind removed (do not remove the fat)
1 teaspoon salt
½ tablespoon cooking oil
2 tablespoons ginger, peeled and sliced
1 stalk *negi* (Welsh onion) or green onion, cut into 2-inch pieces, green and white parts separated

For seasoning
⅔ cup water
⅓ cup sake
⅓ cup soy sauce
3 tablespoons sugar

Directions

1. Make sure to separate any green parts from the core of the white part of the *negi* or green onion.
2. Slice the white parts thinly and soak in cold water for 10 minutes. Drain well and cover with plastic wrap. Set aside.
3. Rub the salt over the pork. If your pork belly block is too large, roll it with the fat side out and tie it with twine. Small blocks may be kept as they are.
4. In a skillet or frying pan, heat the oil over high heat. Brown the pork belly evenly on all sides (about 10 minutes).
5. Combine the seasonings in a pot large enough for the pork to fit.
6. Place the pork in the pot, together with the ginger and green parts of the *negi* or green onion.
7. Add water, just up to the surface of the pork, and bring it to a boil.
8. Cover with an *otoshibuta* or aluminum foil.
9. Set the heat to medium low and simmer the pork, turning from time to time, until the liquid is about ¼ inch deep (about 1 hour). (At this point, you may set aside and freeze some of the *chasu* broth to be used for seasoning *tonkatsu* ramen.)
10. Remove the *otoshibuta* and continue cooking until almost no liquid is left. Be careful not to scorch the pork but if you can, use the heat of the pot to caramelize the surface of the pork. Or remove the meat from the pot and use a propane torch to sear its surface.
11. Cut the pork as thinly as possible. To store, allow it to cool and pack it in an airtight container. It keeps for 5 days in the refrigerator, and for 3 weeks in the freezer.
12. Serve in soups, ramen noodles, rices, and more.

Sushi

In Japan, sushi refers to vinegar rice with raw fish or other basic ingredients wrapped in nori or seaweed "paper." Another version, *nigiri*, is a hand-shaped bite-sized portion of rice with a dash of wasabi and a thin slice of raw fish on top. The origin of sushi is traced back to Southeast Asia, where fish was stored in rice a means of preservation. Through China, sushi was eventually introduced in Japan, during the 8th century. It was a street food that could be eaten quickly with the hands, an ancient kind of fast food.

Sushi in America contains strong flavors and complicated ingredients. Compared to the modest and straightforward Japanese sushi, the American versions are big and bold in flavor. Particularly interesting is the way American sushi is rolled "inside out," with the nori inside the roll. This was perhaps done to tone down the nori, which took some time to gain acceptance. Sushi as we know it is served with wasabi and a soy-based dipping sauce as well as other condiments.

Technically, *Sashimi* is not sushi as it does not contain vinegar rice. *Sashimi* is simply raw fish. In the West, however, sushi has been so associated with raw fish (*Sashimi*) that the two are often confused.

Whether authentic or not, sushi are we know it is here to stay and is enjoyed by millions. It is still evolving to suit our tastes and needs and it has become a permanent part of American food culture.

Here are some basics in making sushi.

Basic Equipment
- sushi rolling mat
- sharp, non-serrated knife
- rice cooker
- plastic wrap
- cutting board

Basic Ingredients
- nori (edible sheets of dried seaweed)
- sushi rice
- raw fish and other seafood (should always be *sashimi*-grade), meat, vegetables, fruit
- sushi condiments (there is a wide variety including soy sauce, wasabi, pickled ginger, mayonnaise, Sriracha, and many more)

Basic Steps in Making Sushi

1. Prepare the nori sheet

Line the rolling mat with a sheet of plastic wrap (this will help in shaping and storing the roll). Place one full sheet of sushi nori on the lined sushi rolling mat, shiny side down.

2. Spread with sushi rice

Cover the nori sheet with prepared sushi rice, leaving the last inch and a half (away from you) bare. Use plastic gloves or moisten your hands with a solution of water and a little vinegar called *tezu* to prevent the rice from sticking.

*NOTE: **To make an inside-out roll,** cover the rice layer with a sheet of plastic wrap. Lifting with the bottom plastic wrap, turn over the nori onto the bamboo rolling mat. Remove top plastic wrap.*

3. Place the filling

Place ingredients for the filling crosswise over the rice-covered nori.

4. Roll

Fold the mat over, to roll the sushi. Apply firm pressure while rolling to make a tight roll.

5. Tighten the roll

Moisten the flap of uncovered nori and roll over it to seal. Repeat rolling to tighten the roll, if necessary. Be careful not to roll the plastic wrap into the sushi.

6. Slice the roll

Use a sharp, non-serrated knife and run cold water over the blade to keep the nori and rice from sticking. Do not use a sawing motion as this would tear the nori. To get even slices, begin slicing at the center of the roll then proceed to cut each piece at the center as well. Cut into 8 small pieces, or 6 larger pieces.

Sliced Raw Fish (Sashimi)

Serves: 4
Preparation Time: 15 minutes
Cooking Time: 0 minutes

Ingredients
1 pound fish (salmon, tuna, snapper, yellowtail, etc.),
must be fresh, *Sashimi*-grade
1 carrot, grated, for garnish
1 *daikon*, grated, for garnish
Soy sauce
Wasabi
Sushi ginger or *gari*

Directions

1. Freeze the fish so it is firm enough to cut thinly.
2. Use a very sharp, non-serrated knife to remove the skin.
3. Cut into ¼-inch thick pieces, about the size of a domino. Your knife should be sharp enough to prevent using a sawing motion that will destroy the flesh.
4. Arrange on a platter and garnish with grated *daikon* and carrot.
5. Serve with soy sauce, wasabi, and sushi ginger or *gari*.

Thick Sushi Roll (Futomaki)

Serves: 2-3
Preparation Time: 30 minutes plus 30 minutes cooling time
Cooking Time: 15 minutes (for sushi rice)

Ingredients
3 sheets nori
15-20 large shrimp, cooked
3 pieces imitation crab sticks, halved lengthwise
⅓ cup carrot, finely grated
1 small Japanese cucumber, cut into strips
1 avocado, pitted, peeled, cut into strips
2 leaves romaine lettuce, shredded
4 cups cooked rice, seasoned with sushi vinegar
¼ cup rice vinegar
Wasabi, soy sauce, and sushi ginger (*gari*), as condiments

Sushi rice
3 cups sushi rice (shari)
4 ¼ cups sushi vinegar (recipe below)

Sushi vinegar
3 ½ cups water
½ cup of rice vinegar (do not use any other vinegar)
2 tablespoons white sugar
2 teaspoons refined salt

Vinegar water for dipping hands (Tezu)
¼ cup water
2 teaspoon rice vinegar

Directions
For sushi vinegar
1. Combine all the sushi vinegar ingredient in pot and warm it on the stovetop over medium heat. Stir until the well dissolved. (You may also heat the vinegar solution in the microwave.)
2. Put the rice in a fine mesh strainer and wash under cold running water until the rinsing water runs clear. Drain well.

Sushi Rice - on the stovetop
3. Place the rice in a heavy-bottomed pot and add the water. Make sure the rice surface is level. Bring it to a boil, reduce the heat to minimum and cover the pot. f the boiling liquid overflows, remove the lid for it to go down and replace the lid immediately. Allow the rice to absorb all the water. Watch out for scorching. If you smell the rice burning, immediately remove it from the heat and allow it to cook in residual heat. The rice is done when all water has been absorbed.

Sushi rice - using a rice cooker

4. Place the washed rice grains in the rice cooker pot and add the 3 ½ cups of water. Cook according to the rice cooker's instructions (usually you just press the "cook" button).
5. Transfer the cooked rice to a *hangiri,* or a large mixing bowl, and place it in the refrigerator to cool. At this stage, fillers can be prepared while waiting for rice to cool down.
6. Make sure the rice is completely cool, as the center may still be hot.
7. Pour the vinegar mixture over the rice and mix it into the rice with your hands.

To make the roll

8. As you will make 3 rolls, divide all the ingredients into 3.
9. Follow the steps for making sushi.
10. In placing the filling:
    - Arrange 5-6 shrimp in a row about 2" from the close edge.
    - Add a row of sea sticks, then a row of shredded lettuce.
    - On top of the shrimp, place slices of avocado and shredded, stacked like logs of wood.
11. Cut each roll into 8 slices. Serve with soy sauce, wasabi and pickled ginger.

Smoke Salmon Philly Roll Sushi

Serves: 2
Preparation Time: 15 minutes
Cooking Time: 0 minutes

Ingredients
2 strips of cream cheese, 8x¼ inches (cut from the block)
3 ounces smoked salmon
2-4 narrow strips cucumber, to fit 8x¼ inches
2 *nori* sheets
1 cup sushi rice

Directions
1. Follow all the steps for making sushi to make about 16 rolls (8 slices each).
2. Serve.

Dragon Roll

Serves: 2-4
Preparation Time: 1 hour
Cooking Time: 0 minutes

Ingredients
For filling
2 avocados, halved, pitted, peeled, sliced thinly crosswise
½ lemon (optional), to squeeze on avocado to prevent browning
2 nori sheets, cut in half crosswise
2 cups prepared sushi rice
1 Japanese cucumber, pitted, cut lengthwise into 8 pieces
8 precooked shrimp tempura

⅛ cup fish roe or *tobiko,* plus more for garnish
Grilled eel *or unagi* (optional)

For toppings
Spicy mayo (Japanese mayo mixed with Sriracha or hot
sauce to taste)
Unagi Sauce (store-bought)
Green onion, sliced for garnish

Directions
1. Gently press the avocado slices with your fingers and then with the side of a knife to make them malleable. Sprinkle with lemon, if using.
2. Follow the steps for making sushi. You'll be rolling it inside out.
3. After turning the roll inside out, put the cucumber strips, shrimp tempura, *tobiko* and *unagi* (optional) at the bottom end of the nori sheet.
4. Roll it up. After you are done rolling, BEFORE CUTTING, place the avocado slices on top to look like a dragon's "scales."
5. Cover with plastic wrap and place the mat over the roll. Squeeze gently to make the avocado wrap over the top of the roll.
6. Cut the roll into 8 slices.
7. Top each slice with a bit of roe. Drizzle with spicy mayo and sprinkle sliced green onions
8. Serve with *unagi* sauce.

Nigiri Sushi

Serves: 6
Preparation Time: 30 minutes plus 1 hour freezing time
Cooking Time: 0 minutes

Ingredients
4-6 ounce piece sushi-grade tuna or salmon
About 3 cups prepared sushi rice
Wasabi
Tezu solution, for washing hands

Directions
1. If using salmon, cover the fish with salt and leave it for 1 hour.
2. Rinse off the salt and put the salmon into the freezer until it is completely frozen.
3. Defrost until it is easy to slice.
4. Slice the fish very thinly, about ¼ inch thick and the size of a domino.
5. Dip hands into the *tezu*.

6. Take a scoop of sushi rice to fit your fist. Pack the rice in your fist to make a small rectangle of sushi rice.
7. Dab one side of the fish slice with wasabi and place it, wasabi side down, on the sushi rectangle.
8. Serve with more wasabi, soy sauce, and sushi ginger.

Vegetarian Nigiri

Serves: 6
Preparation Time: 30 minutes
Cooking Time: 0 minutes

Ingredients
Sushi rice
1 small zucchini, sliced very thinly (paper thin)
1 slice small green *shiso* or *perilla*, cut lengthwise and in small diagonal strips
¼ *nori* seaweed, cut into about ¼-inch wide strips
Wasabi
Salt
Sushi vinegar
Hot sauce

Directions

1. Sprinkle the zucchini slices generously with salt. Rub it in, and leave it to sit until the turnip has wilted. Rinse and drain, and squeeze out the water.
2. In a wok, warm the oil and quickly stir-fry the zucchini. Remove from wok and place on paper towel to absorb excess fat.
3. Take a scoop of sushi rice to fit your fist. Pack the rice in your fist to make a small rectangle.
4. Smear on a dab of wasabi paste, and place piece of *shiso* leaf on top.
5. Dip 2-3 slice of zucchini in sushi vinegar, lay it on the rice and adjust the shape.
6. Wrap a strip of nori like a belt around its width, tucking the ends underneath.
7. If desired, place a dab of hot sauce on top and serve.

Vegetable Maki

Serves: 6-8
Preparation Time: 30 minutes
Cooking Time: 0 minutes

Ingredients
1 package nori roasted seaweed sheets
2 carrots, peeled and sliced lengthwise into narrow strips
1 cucumber, pitted and sliced lengthwise into narrow strips
1 avocado, halved, pitted and cut into narrow strips
Cream cheese (block form), cut into narrow strips
Soy sauce
Wasabi for serving
Sesame seeds

Directions

1. Follow the steps to making sushi up to step 3.
2. For the filling, place a carrot strip, cucumber strip, cream cheese, and avocado across the rice bed.
3. Proceed with the rest of the steps in making sushi.
4. Garnish each piece with sesame seeds.
5. Serve with soy sauce for dipping and wasabi.

Spicy Tuna Maki

Serves: 4-6
Preparation Time: 15 minutes
Cooking Time: 0 minutes

Ingredients
4 sheets nori, cut in half crosswise
2 cups sushi rice
Sushi ginger
Wasabi
Soy sauce

For filling
5 ounces ahi tuna (yellowfin or bigeye), *Sashimi*-grade,
finely chopped
2 tablespoons green onions, minced
2 tablespoons mayonnaise
1 tablespoon hot sauce

Directions

1. Combine the ingredients for the filling in a bowl and mix well.
2. Follow the **steps for making sushi** up to step 3.
3. For the filling, spoon a thin line of the tuna mixture down the center of the rice.
4. Proceed up to step 5 (do not cut yet).
5. Before cutting, remove the plastic wrap and set the roll aside, covering with a damp cloth while you work to finish the remaining rolls.
6. Cut the roll in half, then into thirds so each roll results in 6 pieces.
7. Serve with sushi ginger, wasabi, and soy sauce.

California Maki

Serves: 8-10
Preparation Time: 30 minutes
Cooking Time: 0 minutes

Ingredients
5 sheets nori
1 large cucumber, peeled, seeded, cut lengthwise into long strips
2-3 avocados, halved, pitted and cut into thin strips
Freshly squeezed lemon juice
Imitation crab sticks, cut lengthwise
Wasabi
Sesame seeds, if desired

Directions

1. Sprinkle the avocado with lemon juice to prevent browning.
2. Follow the steps for making sushi for an inside-out roll, up to step 3.
3. For filling, arrange the strips of avocado and cucumber along the center of the rice, and top with crab meat.
4. Proceed with succeeding steps up to step 5 (do not cut yet)
5. Wrap the plastic wrap around the roll and set aside until ready to cut. Refrigerate for longer storage. Repeat with remaining nori sheets to make additional rolls.
6. Roll in sesame seeds if desired. Cut into 6-8 rolls as desired.
7. Serve with wasabi, soy sauce, and sushi ginger.

Soups and Broths

Basic Japanese Stock (Dashi)

Yields 3 ¾ to 7 ¾ cups
Preparation Time: 5 minutes plus 30 minutes soaking time
Cooking Time: 15 minutes

Dashi stock and bonito flakes

Ingredients
1 4x5 inch kelp (*kombu*), wiped clean but not washed
3 cups packed dried bonito flakes (*katsuobushi*) or dried and smoked skipjack tuna and sardine flakes
4-8 cups water, depending on desired strength of flavor

Directions

1. Place the water in a pot or saucepan.
2. Make a couple of slits on the *kombu* and soak it in the water for at least 30 minutes (although 3-8 hours is ideal).
3. Gently bring it to a boil, skimming off any oil or scum.
4. Remove the *kombu* just before water begins to boil. (Set it aside to make rice seasoning.)
5. Turn off the heat and allow the water to cool.
6. Add the bonito flakes and bring it to a boil again.
7. Simmer for just 30 seconds, and turn off the heat. The flakes will sink to the bottom. Let it stand for 10 minutes.
8. Line a sieve with a thick piece of paper towel and strain the broth, gently squeezing out the *Dashi*. (Keep the flakes for rice seasoning).
9. Keeps for 1 week refrigerated or for 3 weeks frozen.

Basic Ramen (Tonkotsu and Torigara) Soup Stock

Serves: 5-7
Preparation Time: 20 minutes
Cooking Time: 120 minutes

Ingredients
2 pounds pork leg bones, cut and washed with warm water (For chicken or *Torigara* soup stock, substitute this with 1 pound of chicken bones with flesh to make a total of 2 ½ pounds)
1 ½ pounds chicken breast, washed with warm water, blood clots removed
½ pound pork trotters, washed well with warm water
1 gallon of water
2-3 cloves garlic
1 stalk green onion, cut into about 3 pieces per stalk

Directions

1. Place all the cleaned bones in a pressure cooker (check your manual as not all pressure cookers work the same way) and fill it with about a gallon of water. The water should not reach up to more than ⅔ of the pot's height, it should just cover the bones.
2. Bring it to a boil, uncovered, and remove any scum (optional).
3. Add the green onion and garlic cloves. Cover.
4. Reduce the heat to low. If you're using an electric stove, you may transfer the whole pot to a second burner with a lower setting. Be careful that you do not get scalded by the steam. Pressure cook for 30 minutes.
5. Let the pot cool, or submerge it in a basin of water for faster cooling.
6. Remove the lid. Mix the contents thoroughly, mashing the vegetables and meat for more flavor. Add water, if needed.
7. Replace the lid and pressure cook for another 30 minutes.
8. After the pressure has gone done, stir and mash again as thoroughly as you can. Repeat two more times, for a total of 120 minutes of intermittent cooking and mixing/mashing.
9. The resulting stock is shimmery, with meat and bones reduced to fragments. You may boil another 30 to 60 minutes, if desired and time allows.
10. Strain out any solids (may be kept for other recipes).
11. Freeze any unused stock as this spoils easily.

Japanese Seafood Soup (Nabe)

Serves: 4
Preparation Time: 5 minutes
Cooking Time: 20-30 minutes

Ingredients
Water to make broth (about 4-8 cups) or ready-made *dashi* stock
1 cup dried boiled anchovy (optional if using ready-made *Dashi* stock)
1 piece *kombu* or kelp (optional if using ready-made *Dashi* stock)
1 medium onion, sliced

1 cup shiitake mushrooms, cored and cut into bite-sized pieces
½ cup *enoki* mushrooms, roots cut off and washed
½ cup green onions, each cut into 4 pieces of equal length
½ head Napa cabbage, cut into large pieces
1 cup firm tofu, cubed
1 pound shrimp, deveined, clean and shelled
½ pound cod fillet or fillet of any fish of choice

For dipping sauce
2 tablespoons green onion, chopped
1-2 tablespoons green Thai chili, chopped
1 cup cold water
¼ cup white vinegar
1 cup soy sauce

Directions
1. Fill a 4-quart pot about ¾ full with water or *dashi* stock.
2. Drop in the anchovies and *kombu*.
3. Bring it to a boil. Reduce the heat and allow it to boil for 10 minutes.
4. Remove it from the heat and scoop out the anchovies and *kombu* from the broth.
5. Add all the vegetables, tofu, and seafood to the broth.
6. Bring it to a boil again and continue the shrimp have changed color.
7. While cooking the soup, combine the ingredients for the sauce in a bowl and set it aside.
8. Serve soup with the dipping sauce.

Miso Soup

Serves: 4
Preparation Time: 5 minutes
Cooking Time: 15 minutes

Ingredients
4 cups *dashi* stock (you may also use granules, following the packaging instructions)
3-4 tablespoons *miso* paste, preferably yellow (but white or red may be used)
1 cup firm tofu, diced and drained on towels
2 green onions, cut into ½-inch pieces

Directions
1. Heat the *dashi* stock in a pot or saucepan, and bring it to a boil.
2. Reduce the heat.
3. Put the *miso* in a strainer, and submerge it in the boiling stock. Press the *miso* through the sieve into the stock.
4. Add the tofu and green onions.
5. Simmer about 3 minutes, and serve.

Salads

Cucumber Salad (Sunomono)

Serves: 4
Preparation Time: 10 minutes
Cooking Time: 0 minutes

Ingredients
2-3 cups cucumber (use Japanese or other thin-skinned cucumbers), sliced as thinly as possible
¼ teaspoon salt
3 tablespoon rice vinegar
1 tablespoon sugar
¼ teaspoon soy sauce
1 teaspoon sesame seeds

Directions

1. Add salt to the sliced cucumbers and mix well. Let them sit for 5 minutes.
2. Meanwhile, combine the vinegar, sugar, and soy sauce in a small bowl until the sugar is completely dissolved. Set aside.
   Drain away all the liquid, squeezing as much as you can from cucumbers.
3. Add the vinegar mixture and sesame seeds to the prepared cucumbers and mix well.

Daikon Salad

Serves: 3-4
Preparation Time: 10 minutes
Cooking Time: 0 minutes

Ingredients
1 ½ tablespoon soy sauce
1 ½ tablespoon rice vinegar
1 ½ tablespoon sesame oil

1 teaspoon sugar

¼ *daikon* (white radish) peeled and spiralized or julienned finely

1 carrot, peeled and spiralized or julienned finely

1 tablespoon black sesame seeds

Roasted seaweed (*nori*), thinly sliced

Directions

1. Whisk together the soy sauce, vinegar, sesame oil, and sugar in a bowl.
2. Add the vegetables and mix well.
3. Serve garnished with sesame seeds and *nori*.

Seaweed (Wakame) Salad

Serves: 2
Preparation Time: 10 minutes
Cooking Time: 0 minutes

Ingredients
½ cup dried, salted *wakame* seaweed
Kaiware radish sprouts or garden cress for garnish, optional
Toasted white sesame seeds for garnish

For dressing
1 tablespoon soy sauce
1 tablespoon vinegar
1 tablespoon *dashi* water
½ teaspoon sugar
1 tablespoon olive oil or sesame oil
½ teaspoon ginger, peeled and grated
½ teaspoon garlic, grated (optional)

Directions

1. Rinse the *wakame* under running water. Squeeze and soak in a bowl of water for 2-3 minutes.
2. Squeeze again and drop into a sieve submerged in a pot of hot water to blanch (about 2 seconds).
3. Lift the *wakame* out of the hot water and immediately pour cold water over it to cool it down quickly. Squeeze out the water.
4. Slice the *wakame* thinly. Set it aside.
5. Whisk together the ingredients for the dressing in a bowl until the sugar is dissolved. Pour the dressing over the *wakame* salad. Add sesame seeds to taste. Mix well.
6. Top with radish sprouts or garden cress, if desired.
7. Mix the dressing again and drizzle it over the salad.

Noodles

Pork Bone (Tonkotsu) Ramen

Serves: 1
Preparation Time: 5 minutes
Cooking Time: 5 minutes

Ingredients
For seasoning sauce
2 tablespoons soy sauce
Dashi to taste
½-1 teaspoon sugar
½ teaspoon *chasu* broth, or to taste (optional)
MSG or fish sauce, if desired, to taste
Dash white pepper powder (optional)
1 teaspoon *mirin* (optional)

To assemble ramen

Ramen noodles (Sapporo, Hakata or Cantonese egg noodles), fresh, frozen, or dried

1 ½-2 cups basic ramen soup stock

1 ½ tablespoons seasoning sauce, or according to taste

NOTE: Use plain salt instead if you do not want soy sauce in your broth and you want a more basic flavor

2 thin slices chashu

½ slice marinated runny yolk boiled egg

Scallions, finely chopped

Black garlic sauce (*mayu*)

Other optional toppings

Fermented bamboo shoot (*menma*), store-bought

Nori (seaweed paper), shredded

Whole kernel corn

Bean sprouts

Wood ear

Directions

To assemble the ramen

1. Prepare the noodles according to the packaging instructions and place a handful (or your own estimate of what would be enough for one serving) in a ramen bowl or soup bowl.
2. Combine the seasoning sauce ingredients in a small bowl.
3. Heat up the basic ramen soup stock to boiling and stir in the seasoning sauce (or plain salt, if preferred). Adjust the taste by adding more seasoning sauce, salt, or more broth, as desired.
4. Pour this hot seasoned stock over the noodles.
5. Top with *chasu*, runny yolk boiled egg, and chopped green onions.
6. Add more toppings, as desired.
7. Drizzle with *mayu* or black garlic oil and serve.

Stir Fried Thick White Noodles (Yaki Udon)

Serves: 3
Preparation Time: 5 minutes
Cooking Time: 15 minutes

Ingredients
2 packages udon noodles
2 tablespoons vegetable oil
½ pound pork belly, cut into bite-sized pieces NOTE: You may substitute other meats, seafood or vegetables of choice
1 small onion, sliced
1 cup cabbage, cut into bite-sized pieces
1 medium carrot, julienned
2 shiitake mushrooms, destemmed and sliced
2 green onions, 2 inches of the tips set aside, the rest cut into 2-inch pieces
3 tablespoons *mentsuyu* or leftover *sukiyaki* sauce

1 teaspoon soy sauce
Freshly ground black pepper, to taste
3 tablespoons bonito flakes or *katsuobushi*

Directions
1. Prepare the noodles according to the packaging instructions. Frozen noodles should be boiled to loosen them, then rinsed and drained.
2. Heat the oil in a wok or frying pan over medium heat, and sauté the pork until browned.
3. Add the onion and cook until translucent (about 2-5 minutes).
4. Add the cabbage, carrots, shiitake, and green onion. Cook until the vegetables are wilted.
5. Add the noodles, *mentsuyu*, soy sauce, and black pepper, and mix well.
6. Adjust the flavor with more seasonings, as needed.
7. Transfer to a serving dish and top with bonito flakes and chopped green onion tips.

Stir-Fried Noodles with Meat and Vegetables (Yaki Udon)

Serves: 3
Preparation Time: 10 minutes
Cooking Time: 20 minutes

Ingredients
2 tablespoons vegetable oil
1 pound boneless chicken breast, cut into bite-sized pieces
1 small onion, sliced
1 cup snow peas
1 cup bean sprouts
½ cup shiitake mushrooms, destemmed and sliced///
Freshly ground black pepper, to taste
½ cup *Yaki Udon* sauce (recipe below, or ready mix) or *mentsuyu*, divided
1 package *Yaki Udon* noodles

Yaki Udon sauce
½ cup light soy sauce or _usukuchi_
1 teaspoon dark soy sauce or _koikuchi_
2 teaspoons sugar
2 teaspoons salt

Directions
1. To prepare _yaki udon_ sauce, combine the sauce ingredients in a saucepan. Bring it to a boil and simmer it over low heat for about 10 minutes. Let it cool. Will keep for about 2 weeks in the refrigerator. Set aside ½ cup for this recipe.
2. Heat the oil in a wok or frying pan over medium-high heat, and sauté the chicken until cooked through.
3. Add the onion and cook until translucent (about 2-5 minutes).
4. Add the snow peas, mushrooms, and bean sprouts. Cook until the vegetables are wilted.
5. Season with black pepper.
6. Add ¼ cup _yaki udon_ sauce.
7. Before adding the noodles, rinse them with warm water to loosen them, and drain.
8. Reduce the heat and add the noodles, stirring constantly to loosen noodles and prevent charring at the bottom of wok or frying pan.
9. Add the remaining ¼ cup of _yaki udon_, adjusting the amount to taste. Serve immediately, garnished with dried seaweed powder and pickled ginger.

Hotpot Beef with Noodles and Vegetables (Sukiyaki)

Serves: 4
Preparation Time: 10 minutes
Cooking Time: 3-5 minutes

Ingredients

1 pound beef tenderloin or sirloin, very thinly sliced

2 tablespoons beef suet, oil, or butter

1 package *shirataki* (*konjac* yam) or cellophane noodles, washed, drained, and cut into 3-inch pieces

8 shiitake mushrooms, destemmed

1 enoki mushroom, trimmed

1 leek, cut into 2-inch pieces

½ head Chinese cabbage, cut into 2-inch pieces, stalks separated from leaves

1 bunch chrysanthemum leaves (*shungiku*); or other leafy greens; torn from stalk

1 grilled tofu, cut into bite-sized pieces

4 pasteurized eggs (fresh and preferably free-range)

Sukiyaki sauce

⅓ cup soy sauce

3 tablespoons sake

5 tablespoons sugar

¾ cup water

Directions

1. Follow the packaging instructions for the noodles. Some may need to be parboiled to remove an offensive odor. Submerge them in cold water in a pot and bring it to a boil. Immediately remove the noodles from the boiling water, drain and submerge in cool water. Drain again.

2. To pasteurize your own eggs, submerge them in water at 140°F for 4 minutes (This is optional if you are sure that the eggs are fresh and you are used to eating raw egg). Remove them from the hot water.

3. Combine the *sukiyaki* sauce ingredients in a bowl. Set it aside.

4. Preheat an electric pan or skillet on the table for cooking ingredients. The meal is served hot, served straight from the pan.
5. Arrange all ingredients on a large serving platter beside the skillet.
6. Add the suet, oil, or butter to the skillet and fry the beef just until it is no longer pink.
7. Push the beef to one side and pour in 2-3 tablespoons of *sukiyaki* sauce.
8. When the sauce begins to boil, add the other ingredients. Traditionally, these are arranged in the skillet in an orderly manner; bunching each type of ingredient in a section of the pan.
9. Start adding the tofu, mushrooms, and cabbage stalks.
10. Next, add the noodles, making sure to place them away from the beef as the shirataki can cause the beef to toughen. Add the leafy greens and onions last, and more sauce, if needed.
11. Place a lid over the skillet and let it simmer for 3 to 5 minutes.
12. Meanwhile, crack one egg per person in a bowl and beat.
13. *Sukiyaki* is eaten by dipping ingredients from the hotpot in raw beaten egg.
14. Make sure the liquid does not dry up. Add more sauce or hot water to the pan when needed.
15. Leftover *sukiyaki* broth is traditionally saved to make udon.

Teriyaki (Soy-Glazed Dishes)

Chicken Teriyaki

Serves: 4
Preparation Time: 5 minutes
Cooking Time: 10 minutes

Ingredients
2 boneless, skinless chicken breasts
Freshly ground black pepper
2 teaspoons vegetable oil
2 green onions, green and white parts, sliced

Teriyaki sauce
¾ cup soy sauce
¼ cup light brown sugar, packed
1 tablespoon rice wine vinegar
1 tablespoon ginger, grated
2 cloves garlic, minced

For slurry (optional)

2 teaspoons water

1 teaspoon cornstarch

Directions

1. Mix the *teriyaki* sauce ingredients together in a bowl. Set it aside.
2. Place the chicken breasts on a cutting board, smooth side facing up. Cover with plastic wrap and pound to flatten them to ½-inch thickness. Cut each piece in half. Season evenly with freshly ground pepper.
3. Heat the oil in a large pan over medium-high heat. Cook the chicken until golden brown (about 3 to 4 minutes on each side).
4. Pour the *teriyaki* sauce mixture over the chicken. Do not stir. Allow the chicken to absorb the sauce as it cooks. Flip the chicken pieces over, if needed. Ensure that the chicken is evenly cooked and that there are no pink areas, especially inside.
5. Remove the chicken pieces with tongs and transfer them to a serving dish.
6. Heat the sauce in the pan 3 to 5 minutes longer for a thin sauce.
7. For a thicker sauce, whisk together the slurry ingredients in a bowl. Whisk the sauce while pouring in the slurry. Keep mixing for about 30 seconds, until thickened. Remove from the heat.
8. Pour the sauce over the chicken.
9. Best served with steamed rice.

Tofu Teriyaki

Serves: 3
Preparation Time: 5 minutes plus 10 minutes marinating time
Cooking Time: 15 minutes

Ingredients
1 (14 ounce) package extra firm tofu, drained and sliced into bite-sized cubes
Oil for frying
¾ cup *teriyaki* sauce
2 shallots, thinly sliced
2 green onions, chopped, divided

For slurry
1 teaspoon cornstarch
2 teaspoons water

Directions

1. Dry the tofu by wrapping it in paper towels.
2. After drying the tofu, let it marinate in the *teriyaki* sauce for 10 minutes. Drain, saving the sauce for later.
3. Heat the oil in a non-stick pan over medium heat.
4. Fry the tofu slices until they are crispy and golden on all sides. Expect the oil to splatter because of moisture from the marinade.
5. Remove the fried tofu from the pan and drain it on paper towels.
6. Drain any oil from the pan in excess of 1 teaspoon.
7. Sauté the shallots and half the chopped green onions. Cook until fragrant (about 2 minutes).
8. Add the *teriyaki* sauce and let it simmer.
9. Mix together the ingredients for the slurry and add it to pan, stirring the sauce continuously. Turn off the heat as soon as the sauce thickens.
10. Pour the sauce over the tofu and garnish with the remaining chopped green onion.
11. Serve with steamed rice.

Steak Teriyaki

Serves: 4
Preparation Time: 5 minutes plus 1 hour marinating time
Cooking Time: 30 minutes

Ingredients
1 ½ pounds flank or skirt steak
Olive oil
Cooked rice and steamed vegetable for serving.

For marinade
⅓ cup *mirin*
⅓ cup *sake*
⅓ cup soy sauce
1 tablespoon sugar
1 tablespoon fresh ginger, grated

Directions

1. Combine the ingredients for the marinade in a bowl and transfer it to a shallow container or resealable bag.
2. Marinate the steak for one hour to overnight. Keep it chilled, and remove it from the refrigerator an hour before cooking.
3. Drain off the marinade into a saucepan. Bring it to a boil.
4. Reduce the heat and simmer until the marinade is reduced to a thin glaze (about 10 minutes).
5. To grill, oil the grates and preheat the grill to high heat. Or heat up a large cast-iron pan over high heat.
6. Pat the steaks dry and rub evenly with olive oil.
7. Sear the meat on the grill or in the pan until one side is well browned (3-5 minutes).
8. Flip over to sear the other side, while basting with the *teriyaki* marinade.
9. After cooking the meat to the desired doneness, remove it from the heat.
10. Let it rest for 10-15 minutes. Keep the sauce warm.
11. After cooling, divide the steak by cutting it thinly along the grain.
12. Slice each half diagonally, this time against the grain, in thin (¼-inch thick) slices.
13. Arrange the slices on a serving plate.
14. Pour the *teriyaki* sauce over the steak slices and serve over rice and steamed vegetables.

Hibachi and Teppanyaki (Grilled Dishes)

Hibachi Vegetables and Sprouts

Serves: 4
Preparation Time: 15 minutes
Cooking Time: 20 minutes

Ingredients
1 tablespoon vegetable oil
½ teaspoon sesame oil
1 large white onion, sliced into slivers
1 large zucchini, quartered
1 cup shiitake mushrooms, destemmed and sliced
1 tablespoon butter
2 tablespoons soy sauce
Salt and pepper, to taste

For bean sprouts
1 tablespoon butter
3 cups bean sprouts
1 tablespoon soy sauce
½ teaspoon sesame oil

Directions
1. Prepare all the ingredients in advance and have them lined up for quick succession in cooking and to maximize use of heat and flavors in the pan or skillet, which serves as your "*hibachi*" or grill.
2. Heat a large heavy skillet or large wok over medium-high heat.

For vegetables

3. Heat the vegetable oil and sesame oil in warmed skillet.

4. Add the onion, zucchini, mushrooms, butter, soy sauce, salt, and pepper, and sauté until the veggies are tender (about 5-10 minutes).

5. Transfer the cooked vegetables to serving dish.

6. Do not clean the pan. The oils and seasonings left on the skillet will add to the overall flavor of the next dish. Keep it warm and follow immediately with the next dish. You may need to scrape off charred bits, if any.

For bean sprouts

7. Melt the butter in the same skillet and add the bean sprouts. Sauté for 1minute.

8. Drizzle with soy sauce and sesame oil as you sauté until the sprouts are translucent but still crisp (about 1 minute).

Beef and Salmon Teppanyaki

Serves: 2
Preparation Time: 5 minutes
Cooking Time: 15 minutes

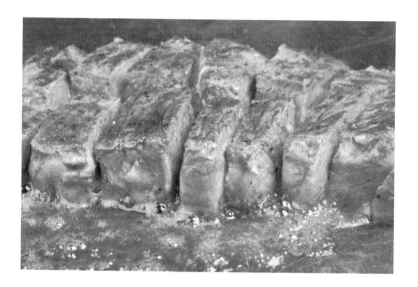

Ingredients

4 ounces beef tenderloin, cut into bite-sized cubes or
thin strips
4 ounces salmon
1-2 tablespoons vegetable or olive oil
1 tablespoon soy sauce
Salt, to taste
Freshly ground pepper
2 tablespoons butter
2 tablespoons *sake*
White pepper, to taste
Flour for coating

Directions

1. Season the salmon and beef (separately) with salt, black pepper, and white pepper.
2. Coat the salmon evenly with flour.
3. Heat a heavy skillet or wok, which will serve as the "*teppan*" or grill.
4. Add the oil and fry the salmon until evenly browned, opaque, and easy to flake with a fork.
5. Move the salmon to the side of the pan and drain off any excess oil. Transfer it to a serving plate. Keep the skillet or wok warm, for cooking the beef.
6. Pan fry the beef in the same skillet until the desired doneness is reached. Season it with freshly ground pepper, and transfer it to the same dish as the salmon.
7. In the same skillet or wok, add butter, *sake*, and white pepper.
8. Turn off the heat and stir to melt the butter.
9. Pour this sauce over the salmon and beef and serve while hot.

Hibachi Chicken and Fried Rice

Serves: 4
Preparation Time: 15 minutes
Cooking Time: 20 minutes

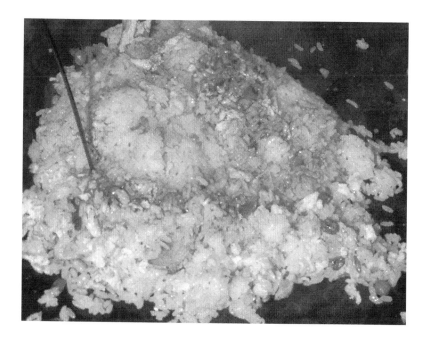

Ingredients
For chicken
1 ½ pounds boneless chicken breast, sliced thinly into bite-sized pieces (may be substituted with beef, pork, or seafood)
1 tablespoon vegetable oil
½ teaspoon sesame oil
1 tablespoon butter
3 tablespoons soy sauce
2 teaspoons fresh lemon juice
Salt and pepper, to taste

For fried rice

2 tablespoons vegetable oil
½ teaspoon sesame oil
1 small white onion, chopped
1 cup bean sprouts
2 large eggs, beaten
Salt and pepper, to taste
4 cups cooked rice, preferably chilled for a few hours or overnight
4 tablespoons butter
½ teaspoon garlic powder
3 tablespoons soy sauce, or to taste
1 tablespoon *sake* (optional)

Directions

1. Prepare all the ingredients in advance and have them lined up for quick succession in cooking and to maximize the use of heat and flavors in the pan or skillet, which serves as your "*hibachi*" or grill.
2. Break the chilled rice apart using your hands or a large spoon, to separate the grains. Set it aside.
3. Heat a large heavy skillet or large wok over medium-high heat.

For chicken

4. Pour the vegetable and sesame oils in the pan.
5. Add the chicken and toss with a spatula while adding the butter, soy sauce, lemon juice, salt, and pepper. Continue sautéing the chicken until it is cooked through (about 6-8 minutes).

6. Transfer the chicken to a serving dish and reserve the skillet (do not clean) for the next dish. The oils and seasonings left on the skillet from the chicken will add to the overall flavor of the next dish. Keep it warm and follow immediately with next dish. You may need to scrape off charred bits, if any.

For fried rice

7. With the same skillet used previously, heat up the oils.
8. Add the chopped onion and sauté until almost tender (about 3-4 minutes).
9. Add the bean sprouts and continue sautéing (about 2 minutes).
10. Move onions and bean sprouts to the side of pan and add the eggs, mixing to scramble as you add them, and seasoning lightly with salt and pepper.
11. Add the rice, butter, and garlic powder, and continue stirring for about 5 minutes. Use a shoveling motion to mix.
12. Add the soy sauce and *sake* and continue cooking, mixing constantly (about 1 to 2 minutes). Adjust the taste with more salt and pepper or soy sauce, as needed.
13. This may be followed with *hibachi* vegetables and sprouts.

Fried Rice, Rice Bowls and Pork Cutlet (Yakimeshi, Donburi and Katsu)

Chicken Fried Rice (Yakimeshi No Tori)

Serves: 4-5
Preparation Time: 5 minutes
Cooking Time: 10 minutes

Ingredients
¼ cup vegetable oil
5 cups cooked rice, preferably chilled overnight
1 clove garlic, minced
2 cups cooked chicken, shredded (may be substituted with pork belly or shrimp)
1 small onion, chopped
½ cup celery, diced
¼ cup bell pepper, diced

½ cup combination of peas, carrots and corn (if not the frozen, be sure to blanch first and drain)
2 eggs, beaten
2 tablespoons soy sauce
Salt, to taste
Dash white pepper

Directions

1. Break up the cooked rice with your hands or a large spoon to loosen the grains. Set it aside.
2. Heat up a wok. A very hot wok is important for cooking fried rice.
3. Add the oil and let it warm for a second or two.
4. Add the rice and garlic, mixing constantly using a "shoveling" motion (This is to keep the rice from sticking to the bottom of the pan).
5. Add the other ingredients EXCEPT eggs, soy sauce, salt, and pepper.
6. Keep "shoveling" until well mixed.
7. Push the rice to one side and drop the beaten eggs into the pan. Let the eggs cook, scrambling them with a spatula. Mix them into the rice.
8. Add the soy sauce, salt, and white pepper and mix well. Serve hot.

Katsu Curry

Serves: 2
Preparation Time: 15 minutes
Cooking Time: 30 minutes

Ingredients
2 pieces cooked *katsu*
2 bowls steamed rice

For the curry sauce
2 tablespoons flour
4-5 teaspoons curry powder
2 tablespoons vegetable oil
2 onions, sliced
5 cloves garlic, chopped
2 medium carrots, peeled and sliced
2 ½ cups chicken stock
2 teaspoons honey or sugar
4 teaspoons soy sauce
1 bay leaf

Directions

1. Combine the flour and curry powder in a bowl. Set it aside.
2. Heat the oil in a non-stick saucepan over medium heat.
3. Sauté the onion and garlic until softened (about 2-5 minutes).
4. Add the carrots and cook, with stirring, over low heat (about 10 minutes).
5. Add flour and curry mixture and stir for 1 minute.
6. While stirring, gradually pour in the stock until combined.
7. Stir in the honey, soy sauce, and bay leaf, and bring it to a boil.
8. Reduce the heat and simmer until the sauce is thickened but pourable (about 20 minutes).
9. Adjust the flavor by adding more curry powder, honey or sugar, or soy sauce, to taste.
10. Strain out the vegetables, if desired, and remove the bay leaf. Blend to a smooth consistency and heat up again. Otherwise, use the sauce as is.
11. Place katsu over rice, and pour curry sauce over it, and serve.

Beef Rice Bowl (Gyudon)

Serves: 1-2
Preparation Time: 5 minutes
Cooking Time: 20 minutes

Ingredients

7 ounces beef, sliced into thin strips or bite-sized pieces
1 small onion, sliced thickly (about ½ inch)
1-2 servings steamed rice, freshly cooked

For sauce
¾ cup water
1 tablespoon sugar
1 tablespoon white wine
1 tablespoon red wine
1 tablespoon *mirin*
2 tablespoons soy sauce
1 tablespoon *dashi*
2 cloves garlic, grated
1 teaspoon ginger, grated

Toppings (optional)
Red pickled ginger or *beni shoga*
Seven spice powder or *shichimi togarashi*

Directions

1. Combine the sauce ingredients in a saucepan and bring it to a boil.
2. Add the onions and cook for 1 minute.
3. Add the beef. Reduce the heat and let it simmer until the beef is done (about 10-15 minutes). Let it cool to develop the flavors, and then reheat (skip this step if you're in a hurry).
4. Pour over the prepared rice and add your choice of toppings (optional).

Deep-Fried Breaded Pork Cutlet (Katsudon)

Serves: 2
Preparation Time: 5 minutes
Cooking Time: 20 minutes

Ingredients
1 medium onion, thinly sliced
2 large eggs, beaten
2 servings steamed white rice, freshly cooked
Green onion, chopped, for garnish

For sauce
½ cup *dashi* stock
2 teaspoons sugar
1 tablespoon soy sauce
2 teaspoons *mirin*

Katsu or breaded cutlet

2 pieces boneless pork chops, pounded to ⅛-inch thickness (may be substituted with chicken breast or thigh, or beef)

Salt and pepper

Flour, for dusting

1 egg, beaten (for coating)

1 cup panko breadcrumbs

Cooking oil, for frying

Directions
1. Whisk together ingredients for sauce in a bowl. Set aside.

For breaded cutlets
2. Place the egg and panko in separate shallow bowls.
3. Season the pork chops with salt and pepper. Dust lightly with flour.
4. Heat up a skillet or wok and add the oil. Test if the oil is hot enough by dropping in a pinch of panko. The panko should sizzle.
5. Dip the pork in the egg, followed by the panko. Press down on the breadcrumbs to make sure they stick well to the pork.
6. Fry the breaded pork until golden brown (about 5 minutes on both sides).
7. Remove from the pan and drain on paper towels. Cut the pork into ½-inch strips, but not all the way to the other one edge, so you can still pick it up as a whole piece.

For sauce and to assemble Katsudon

8. Heat up another wok or skillet over medium heat. Add 1 tablespoon of oil from that used to fry the cutlets.
9. Add the onions and sauté until slightly caramelized.
10. Pour the sauce over the onions and bring it to a boil.
11. Arrange the cutlets over the onions.
12. Reduce the heat to low, and pour the eggs over the meat. Do not stir. At this point, fill 2 *donburi* bowls (or regular bowls) with hot rice and set them aside.
13. When the egg has set, turn off the heat.
14. Place the cutlets with sauce, onions, and egg over steamed rice and garnish with green onion.

Chicken and Egg Rice Bowl (Oyakudon)

Serves: 2
Preparation Time: 10 minutes
Cooking Time: 10 minutes

Ingredients
10 ounces boneless chicken thighs, skin on
¼ teaspoon salt
2 tablespoons *sake*

3 scallions, cut in half

1 large egg, beaten just to break the yolk

For sauce

½ cup *dashi* or chicken stock

2 teaspoons soy sauce

2 teaspoons honey (or 2 teaspoons sugar + 1 teaspoon water)

¼ teaspoon salt

Directions

1. Combine the sauce ingredients in a bowl and set it aside.
2. Season the chicken evenly with ¼ teaspoon salt.
3. Place the chicken pieces on an unheated flat-bottomed pan.
4. Place the pan on the stovetop (do not turn on the heat yet) and weigh down the chicken pieces by placing another heavy pan (or a pot filled with water) over them to keep them flat.
5. Now, turn on the heat to medium. This method allows the chicken to cook evenly and fat to render out. Let the chicken fry until the skin is golden brown (about 7-10 minutes).
6. Remove the chicken from the pan and cut it into bite-sized pieces (It may not thoroughly done at this point).
7. Drain any oil from the pan, leaving just a thin coating and any bits from the chicken.
8. Return the chicken and its juices to the pan. Add the sake and stir-fry until all the liquid has dried up.
9. Add the sauce mixture and bring it to a boil.
10. Sprinkle with scallions and pour in the egg.

11. Cover the pan and reduce the heat to low. Let it cook until the egg is of the desired doneness.
12. Portion over the rice in the bowls, and serve.

Tempura (Battered and Deep-Fried)

Shrimp Tempura

Serves: 2-3
Preparation Time: 20 minutes
Cooking Time: 15 minutes

Ingredients
1 pound large shrimps, shells removed and deveined, tails intact
2 cups panko breadcrumbs
Cooking oil for frying
Tempura sauce or *mentsuyu* for dipping

Basic tempura batter
½ cup all-purpose flour
½ cup cornstarch
1 teaspoon baking powder

½ teaspoon salt

1 teaspoon garlic powder (optional)

1 teaspoon onion powder (optional)

½ teaspoon white pepper (optional)

1 cup ice cold water

Directions

1. Whisk ingredients for the batter in a bowl and keep it refrigerated until use (cold batter contributes to getting crispier results).
2. Place the breadcrumbs in a shallow bowl.
3. To straighten the shrimps or prawns, make a diagonal slit on the undersides. Set them aside.
4. One at a time, dip the shrimp into the cool batter.
5. Next, dip them in the breadcrumbs, making sure to pack the crumbs well onto the surface of the shrimp. Set aside on a platter, and continue until all the shrimps are battered.
6. Heat up oil in a wok or fryer, at least 2 inches deep.
7. While heating the oil, dip the shrimps in batter and breadcrumbs a second time.
8. Drop the shrimps into the hot oil one by one. Do not crowd.
9. Cook until golden brown (about 3 minutes).
10. Drain on paper towels.
11. Serve with tempura sauce or *mentsuyu* for dipping.

Mixed Vegetable Tempura

Serves: 3-4
Preparation Time: 20 minutes
Cooking Time: 15 minutes

Ingredients
1 pound assorted vegetables such as:
Broccoli, cauliflower or green beans, cut in 3-inch lengths
Sweet potatoes, sliced ¼-inch thick
Zucchini or eggplant, cut in 3-inch strips
Carrots, sliced ¼-inch thick
Others: onions, bell pepper, squash, lotus root, mushrooms
Basic tempura batter
2 cups panko breadcrumbs
Oil for frying
Tempura sauce or *mentsuyu* for dipping

Directions

1. Place the breadcrumbs in a shallow bowl.
2. Dip the vegetables in the cool batter.
3. Next, dip them in breadcrumbs, making sure to pack them well.
4. Heat up the oil in a wok or fryer, at least 2 inches deep.
5. While heating the oil, dip the vegetables in batter and breadcrumbs a second time.
6. Drop the vegetables into hot the oil one by one. Do not crowd.
7. Cook until golden brown (about 2-3 minutes), and drain on paper towels.
8. Serve with tempura sauce or *mentsuyu* for dipping.

Dips, Sauces and Condiments

Multi-purpose Sauce (Mentsuyu)

Serves: 3-4
Preparation Time: 5 minutes
Cooking Time: 20 minutes

Ingredients
½ cup soy sauce
½ cup *mirin*
¼ cup *sake*
Handful of dried bonito flakes

Directions
1. Place everything in a pot or saucepan and bring it to a boil.
2. Remove from the heat as soon as it starts to boil, and allow it to cool completely.
3. Strain out the bonito flakes.

4. To use as a dipping sauce, dilute 1:1 sauce to water.
5. For cooking, adjust the amount according to taste.
6. Good for making sauces for noodle dishes or as an alternate dip for tempura.
7. Keeps for 2 weeks in the refrigerator.

Homemade Wasabi Paste Two Ways

Serves: 1-5
Preparation Time: 10-15 minutes
Cooking Time: 0 minutes

Ingredients
From the rhizome
Wasabi root

From horseradish (imitation wasabi)
4 teaspoons horseradish, grated
1 teaspoon Chinese mustard, pounded or pureed
A few drops of soy sauce, according to taste
A few drops vinegar, to taste (enhances pungency)
1 cooked anchovy, chopped finely (optional)

Directions

From the fresh rhizome

1. Wash the wasabi rhizome and let it air dry.
2. Peel about ½ inch around the end.
3. Grate using a fine grater, or special wasabi shark skin grater, enough for 1 serving or more.
4. Shape the resulting paste into a ball and let it stand for about 10 minutes for the flavor to develop.
5. Wrap any leftover in a damp paper towel and then with plastic wrap.

Note: Wasabi is pungent, so be careful not to get it in your eyes. Also, the flavor quickly deteriorates.

To store wasabi root

6. Wrap it in muslin cloth, leaving the cut end exposed.
   Immerse the cut end in a little water and refrigerate. Change the water every 3 days.
   Wasabi will keep this way for about a month.

To make imitation wasabi

7. Combine ingredients thoroughly and adjust flavor accordingly.
8. Store in an airtight jar and refrigerate.
9. A regular condiment for sushi.

Sushi Ginger (Gari)

Yields over 1 ⅓ cups
Preparation Time: 40 minutes
Cooking Time: 5 minutes

Ingredients

1 cup fresh young ginger root, peeled and sliced thinly, preferably young ginger
1 ½ teaspoons sea salt
1 cup rice vinegar
⅓ cup white sugar

Directions

1. Coat the ginger slices well with salt and let stand for 30 minutes.
2. Squeeze out any liquid and place the slices in a glass jar.
3. In a saucepan, stir sugar in vinegar until it is dissolved.

4. Bring it to a boil and immediately pour it into the jar with sliced ginger.
5. Let it cool and place a lid on jar. It keeps for a week, refrigerated.
6. Serve with sushi.

Tempura Sauce

Yields 1 ½ cups
Preparation Time: 5 minutes
Cooking Time: 0 minutes

Ingredients
1 cup *Dashi* stock
¼ cup *mirin*
¼ cup soy sauce
½ tablespoon sugar
¼ cup *daikon* radish, peeled and grated

Directions
1. Mix the ingredients, except the *daikon*, together in a saucepan.
2. Bring it to a boil.
3. Remove it from heat and let it cool down.
4. Add grated the *daikon* and serve.

Soy Dipping Sauce

Yields over ⅓ cup
Preparation Time: 3minutes
Cooking Time: 0 minutes

Ingredients
¼ cup soy sauce
2 tablespoons rice vinegar

Directions
1. Mix the soy sauce and vinegar in a small bowl.
2. Use this as a dip with dumplings or tempura.

Black Garlic Oil (Mayu)

Yields ¼ cup
Preparation Time: 3 minutes
Cooking Time: 0 minutes

Ingredients

¼ cup sesame oil

5 garlic cloves, grated

Directions

1. Combine the sesame oil and garlic in a saucepan and heat it over medium heat. Stir occasionally.
2. When the garlic is browned, reduce the heat to low.
3. Continue cooking until the garlic turns black.
4. Immediately remove from the heat and let it cool.
5. When it is cool, place it in a blender and pulse until it is uniform in color and consistency.
6. Store it in the refrigerator.
7. Drizzle over *tonkatsu* or use it in salad dressings, meat sauces, and dips.

Spicy Dipping Sauce

Yields ¾ cup
Preparation Time: 3minutes
Cooking Time: 0 minutes

Ingredients
⅓ cup rice vinegar
¼ cup green onions, chopped
¼ cup soy sauce
½ teaspoon red pepper, crushed

Directions
1. Mix the ingredients together and let them stand for a few minutes, so the flavor can develop, before serving.
2. May be used for dumplings or tempura.

Ponzu Sauce

Serves: 10
Preparation Time: 3 minutes
Cooking Time: 0 minutes

Ingredients
½ cup soy sauce
¼ cup orange juice
2 tablespoons lemon juice
1 tablespoon water
1 tablespoon mirin
1 teaspoon brown sugar
¼ teaspoon crushed red pepper flakes

Directions
1. Combine all the ingredients in a small bottle, and shake to combine.
2. Store it in the refrigerator.
3. Drizzle over *gyoza,* tempura, or meat dishes.

Desserts

Tempura Ice Cream

Serves: 2-4
Preparation Time: 15 minutes plus 2 hours freezing time
Cooking Time: 2 minutes

Ingredients
1 cup all-purpose flour
1 teaspoon baking soda
1 egg
1 cup ice cold water
1 teaspoon vanilla extract
Vegetable oil to deep fry, should not have flavor
2 cups ice cream, any flavor, completely frozen
Ice cubes
Powdered sugar for dusting (optional)
Chocolate syrup and whipped cream for garnish, if desired

Directions

1. Make scoops of ice cream with an ice cream scoop, and place them on a baking tray. Cover with plastic wrap and freeze for 2 hours to overnight.

For batter

2. Fill a large bowl with ice cubes.
3. Place another smaller bowl in the bowl of ice and sift the flour and baking soda together in that smaller bowl.
4. Beat the egg in another bowl, lightly, until begins to froth.
5. Add the ice-cold water and vanilla to the beaten egg and mix well.
6. Combine the egg and flour mixtures, whisking until just combined. Do not over mix.
7. Preheat the oil for frying, about 2 inches deep, to 350°F and not more than 400°F.
8. Get your frozen ice cream balls out of the freezer. Take one and dip it into the tempura batter.
9. Very carefully drop the ice cream ball into the hot oil and fry it for about 30 seconds. The batter will be pale brown.
10. Serve immediately. Top with chocolate syrup and whipped cream, if desired.

Mochi with Sweet Bean Filling (Daifuku)

Serves: 6
Preparation Time: 30 minutes
Cooking Time: 9 minutes

Ingredients
1 ½ cups *mochiko* sweet rice flour
1 cup sugar
1 ½ cups water
¼ teaspoon salt
2 drops rice vinegar
2 drops red food coloring (optional)
½ can sweet red bean paste

For coating
4 tablespoons potato starch or cornstarch
2 tablespoons sugar

Directions

1. Whisk together the *mochiko*, sugar, water, salt, and rice vinegar in a microwavable bowl.
2. Add the food coloring (optional) and whisk until the batter turns pink.
3. Cover the bowl loosely with plastic wrap, and microwave on high for 9 minutes.
4. Taste a small piece of *mochi*. If it is still grainy, microwave for 1 more minute.
5. Use a cookie scoop to portion the sweet red bean paste into 12 smooth balls.
6. Mix the *mochi* coating ingredients together, and sprinkle half of it onto a large cutting board.
7. Dump the hot *mochi* onto the cutting board.
8. Using the flat edge of a large chef knife, push the *mochi* into an even rectangle shape.
9. Working while the *mochi* is still hot, cut the *mochi* slab evenly into 12 small rectangles.
10. Take one piece and flatten it with your hands. Put a ball of red bean paste in the middle and carefully fold the rectangle corners upward.
11. Pinch the edges around the filling to seal.
12. Dust the bottom and top with the *mochi* coating. Smoothen and place, sealed side down, on a plate or tray.
13. Repeat for the remaining *mochi*. Cover with plastic wrap and store at room temperature.
14. Best eaten the same day.

Conclusion

Japanese dishes are so diverse and exotic, you will always have something new to learn and discover. This cookbook serves only as an introduction to the fascinating world of Japanese-American cuisine.

As you enjoy preparing the dishes and sharing them with family and friends, perhaps you will do your part in helping this kind of cooking to evolve further, happily merging the flavors and techniques of East and West.

Although Japanese takeout in America may not be considered as authentic Japanese cuisine, it still reflects America's dynamic lifestyle and promises more delicious concoctions to come.

Image credits

Tonkotsu Ramen Broth
Public Domain,
https://commons.wikimedia.org/w/index.php?curid=2317
213

Teriyaki Steak
By John Phelan - Own work, CC BY 3.0,
https://commons.wikimedia.org/w/index.php?curid=1813
7838

More Books by Lina Chang

Appendix - Cooking Conversion Charts

1. Measuring Equivalent Chart

Type	Imperial	Imperial	Metric
Weight	1 dry ounce		28g
	1 pound	16 dry ounces	0.45 kg
Volume	1 teaspoon		5 ml
	1 dessert spoon	2 teaspoons	10 ml
	1 tablespoon	3 teaspoons	15 ml
	1 Australian tablespoon	4 teaspoons	20 ml
	1 fluid ounce	2 tablespoons	30 ml
	1 cup	16 tablespoons	240 ml
	1 cup	8 fluid ounces	240 ml
	1 pint	2 cups	470 ml
	1 quart	2 pints	0.95 l
	1 gallon	4 quarts	3.8 l
Length	1 inch		2.54 cm

*   Numbers are rounded to the closest equivalent

2. Oven Temperature Equivalent Chart

T(°F)	T(°C)
220	100
225	110
250	120
275	140
300	150
325	160
350	180
375	190
400	200
425	220
450	230
475	250
500	260

* $T(°C) = [T(°F)-32] * 5/9$

** $T(°F) = T(°C) * 9/5 + 32$

*** Numbers are rounded to the closest equivalent

Made in the USA
San Bernardino, CA
02 January 2017